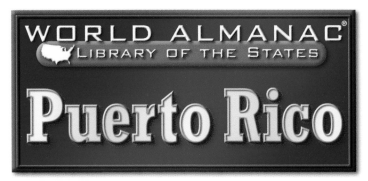

WORLD ALMANAC® LIBRARY OF THE STATES

Puerto Rico

AND OTHER OUTLYING AREAS

by Michael Burgan

WORLD ALMANAC® LIBRARY

Please visit our web site at: **www.worldalmanaclibrary.com**
For a free color catalog describing World Almanac® Library's list of high-quality books
and multimedia programs, call 1-800-848-2928 (USA) or 1-800-387-3178 (Canada).
World Almanac® Library's fax: (414) 332-3567.

Library of Congress Cataloging-in-Publication Data

Burgan, Michael.
    Puerto Rico and other outlying areas / by Michael Burgan.
      p. cm. — (World Almanac Library of the states)
    Includes bibliographical references and index.
    ISBN 0-8368-5158-7 (lib. bdg.)
    ISBN 0-8368-5329-6 (softcover)
    1. Puerto Rico—Juvenile literature. 2. Virgin Islands of the United States—
Juvenile literature. 3. American Samoa—Juvenile literature. 4. Mariana Islands—
Juvenile literature. 5. Guam—Juvenile literature. I. Title. II. Series.
    F1958.3.B874   2003
    972.95—dc21   2002044916

First published in 2003 by
World Almanac® Library
330 West Olive Street, Suite 100
Milwaukee, WI 53212 USA

A Creative Media Applications Production
Design: Alan Barnett, Inc.
Copy editor: Laurie Lieb
Fact checker: Joan Verniero
Photo researcher: Linnette Mathewson
World Almanac® Library project editor: Tim Paulson
World Almanac® Library editors: Mary Dykstra, Gustav Gedatus, Jacqueline Laks Gorman,
 Lyman Lyons
World Almanac® Library art direction: Tammy Gruenewald
World Almanac® Library graphic designers: Scott M. Krall, Melissa Valuch

Photo credits: pp. 4-5 © Bruce Coleman; p. 6 (left) © John Elk III; p. 6 (top right) © John Elk III;
p. 6 (bottom right) © John Elk III; p. 7 (top) © Frank Borges Llosa Photography; p. 7 (bottom)
© Corbis Images; p. 9 © John Elk III; p. 10 © North Wind Picture Archives; p. 11 © North Wind
Picture Archives; p. 12 © Tom Till Photography; p. 13 © AP Photo/Richardo Figueroa; p. 15
© Bruce Coleman; p. 16 © AP/Wide World Photos; p. 17 © AP Photo/Tomas van Houtryve; p. 18
(left) © Bruce Coleman; p. 18 (center) © Stuart Westmoreland/CORBIS; p. 18 (right) © Bruce
Coleman; p. 19 (left) © Bruce Coleman; p. 19 (center) © John Elk III; p. 19 (right) © ArtToday;
p. 21 © Tito Guzman/CORBIS SYGMA; p. 24 © Bruce Coleman; p. 25 © AP/Wide World Photos;
p. 27 © John Elk III; p. 29 (top) Courtesy of Luis Muñoz Marín Foundation, Puerto Rico; p. 29
(bottom) © AP Photo/Lynne Sladky; p. 30 © John Elk III; p. 31 © John Elk III; p. 32 © Photri, Inc.;
p. 33 © Ulrike Welsch; p. 35 © Hulton Archive/Getty Images; p. 37 (left) © AP/Wide World
Photos; p. 37 (right) © AP/Wide World Photos; p. 38 © AP/Wide World Photos; p. 39 © Corbis
Images; p. 40 © Corbis Images; p. 41 © Corbis Images; pp. 42-43 © North Wind Picture
Archives; p. 44 top) © AP/Wide World Photos; p. 44 (bottom) © AP/Wide World Photos; p. 45
(top) © Bruce Coleman; p. 45 (bottom) © AP/Wide World Photos

Printed in the United States of America

1 2 3 4 5 6 7 8 9 07 06 05 04 03

Puerto Rico
and Other Outlying Areas

A Special Relationship

With its sunny weather and warm waters, Puerto Rico is a popular vacation spot for many Americans. This island separates the Atlantic Ocean and the Caribbean Sea. It is home for almost four million people, and has a special relationship with the United States. Puerto Ricans are U.S. citizens and can serve in the military, but they do not pay federal taxes or vote in U.S. presidential elections, as the citizens of the fifty states do. Puerto Rico is called a commonwealth — it is part of the United States, yet in some ways it is independent.

Puerto Ricans often debate changing their relationship with the United States. Some would prefer their island to be a state. A small number want total independence. But wherever they stand on this issue, Puerto Ricans are proud of their homeland and its long history. Many of the 3.8 million Puerto Ricans who live on the mainland frequently return to Puerto Rico. They visit friends and relatives, and some settle there when they retire.

Puerto Rico — sometimes called the "isle of enchantment" — is known for its enjoyable weather, tropical foods, and breathtaking scenery. Puerto Ricans also treasure their special culture. Their art, language, and habits blend a Spanish influence, Native American traditions, and the culture of the African slaves who once worked on the island's plantations. Puerto Rico is a small island filled with energy and variety.

Puerto Rico is one of several island territories that are part of the United States. The U.S. Virgin Islands are located near Puerto Rico. Thousands of miles to the west, in the Pacific Ocean, are Guam, American Samoa, and the Northern Mariana Islands. In all of these outlying areas, local customs and culture blend with American-style democracy and a love of freedom.

▶ Map of Puerto Rico showing major cities and waterways.

▼ El Morro Fortress is one of the tourist highlights of San Juan.

N

PUERTO RICO

ATLANTIC OCEAN

- Arecibo
- *Lago de Guajataco*
- Vega Baja
- San Juan
- *Lago La Plata*
- Bayamon
- *Rio La Plata*
- *Rio Grande de Loiza*
- Loiza Aldea
- **CULEBRA I.**
- San Sebastian
- *Lago Carraizo (Loiza)*
- Fajardo
- *Rio Grande de Anasco*
- Orocovis
- Caguas
- Maguabo
- Mayaguez
- Castaner
- San Lorenzo
- Humacao
- Cayey
- San German
- Coamo
- **VIEQUES I.**
- Yauco
- Ponce
- Guayama
- Maunabo

CARIBBEAN SEA

SCALE KEY

0   25 Miles

0   30 Kilometers

⭐ Capital

🛡 Interstate Highways

Fast Facts

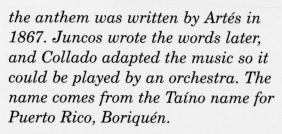

Puerto Rico (PR)

Became a Commonwealth

July 25, 1952

Capital	Population
San Juan	434,374

Total Population (2000)

3,803,610 — *Between 1990 and 2000, Puerto Rico's population increased 8.1 percent.*

Largest Cities	Population
San Juan	434,374
Bayamón	224,044
Ponce	186,475
Carolina	186,076
Caguas	140,502
Arecibo	100,131
Guaynabo	100,053
Mayagüez	98,434

Land Area

3,425 square miles (8,871 square kilometers)

Motto

Joannes Est Nomen Eius — *Latin for "John is his name"*

National Anthem

"La Borinqueña" *by Felix Astol Artés, Ramón Collado, and Manuel Fernández Juncos; adopted in 1952. The music for the anthem was written by Artés in 1867. Juncos wrote the words later, and Collado adapted the music so it could be played by an orchestra. The name comes from the Taíno name for Puerto Rico, Boriquén.*

Official Bird

Reinita, or stripe-headed tanager — *Found only in parts of the Caribbean, the reinita has a high-pitched song with some notes too high for people to hear.*

Official Flower

Maga, or Puerto Rican hibiscus

Official Tree

Ceiba, or silk-cotton tree

Unofficial Animal

Coquí — *This tiny frog lives in trees and plants, and often appears in Puerto Rican art. Its chirping croak, which sounds like its name, is heard across the island. Puerto Ricans proud of their heritage say, "I'm as Puerto Rican as a coquí."*

PLACES TO VISIT

El Morro Fortress, *San Juan*

El Morro Fortress is officially known as El Castillo San Felipe del Morro. Construction on this massive fortress began in 1539. The fortress has a splendid view of San Juan Bay, along with secret tunnels and dungeons.

Río Camuy Cave Park, *Arecibo*

Río Camuy has one of the largest underground cave systems in the world. Underground rivers, especially the Camuy, carved out the caves more than one million years ago.

El Yunque Rain Forest, *Palmer*

Officially known as the Caribbean National Forest, El Yunque is the only tropical rain forest under the control of the U.S. National Forest System. Parts of the forest receive up to 200 inches (508 centimeters) of rain per year.

For other places and events, see p. 44.

BIGGEST, BEST, AND MOST

- The Arecibo Observatory, run by Cornell University, has the world's largest radio telescope dish — 1,000 feet (305 meters) wide.

- Puerto Rico has the largest population of all the outlying U.S. areas.

- The Tibes Indian Ceremonial Center is the oldest known cemetery in the West Indies. Skeletons found there date back to A.D. 300.

HISTORIC FIRSTS

- **1533** La Fortaleza, the official home of Puerto Rico's governor, was completed. It is the oldest executive mansion in continuous use in the Western Hemisphere.

- **1990** Puerto Rican native Antonia Novello became the first woman and the first Hispanic to serve as the U.S. surgeon general, holding that position until 1993.

Underwater Light

In a bay near Parguera, a shimmering blue light illuminates the water. The light comes from billions of tiny creatures called dinoflagellates. The creatures emit light as they move. This light production is called bioluminescence. Bioluminescent organisms live in different parts of the ocean, but only where many of them come together, as at Parguera, do they create light visible on the water's surface. Another bioluminescent bay is located off the Puerto Rican island of Vieques.

Pirate Place

Mona Island is home to the biggest lizards in Puerto Rico and rare plants, but no humans live on the island. In the past, however, a variety of people lived on Mona, which is just off the west coast of the main island. Some Taíno Native Americans once lived there, and the Spanish settled there briefly. Mona's most notorious residents were pirates, who rested at the island between voyages. Some people believe treasure is still buried under Mona's sands.

From Colony to Commonwealth

This island [Boriquén] is very lovely and seems very fertile . . . all these islands are very lovely and of good soil but this one seemed best to all.

— *Diego Alvarez Chanca, in a letter to the leaders of Seville, Spain, after Christopher Columbus's voyage to Puerto Rico in 1493*

More than five thousand years ago, Native people of South America and possibly Florida sailed to Puerto Rico and neighboring islands. These first settlers lived close to the coast, mostly fishing for their food. Later, Native Americans called the Arawak came to the island in three different waves. The Igneri, who arrived about A.D. 100, were excellent potters. The Ostionoid came a few hundred years later, followed by the Taíno, the most advanced of the Native settlers. The Taíno called the island *Boriquén,* which means "land of the brave lord."

The Taíno were ruled by chiefs called *caciques.* Women were considered the equal of men and could serve as caciques. The Taíno also had a formal religion with many different gods. They held religious ceremonies and dances in the center of their villages, which could have several thousand people.

For food, the Taíno mostly farmed. Their main crops included sweet potatoes, beans, squashes, corn, and cassava, a root plant they baked into bread. The Taíno also fished and hunted birds. Their craftspeople made pots, and some skilled workers made jewelry out of gemstones and gold.

By the 1400s, the Taíno had one major enemy: the Carib. Native Americans originally from South America, the Carib attacked many Caribbean islands where the Taíno lived. The Taíno defended themselves, but the Carib won most battles. These wars were still raging when the first Spanish explorer reached Puerto Rico's shores.

Beginnings of Spanish Rule

On November 19, 1493, during his second voyage to what Europeans called "the New World," Christopher Columbus

Native Americans of Puerto Rico
Carib
Igneri
Ostionoid
Taíno

DID YOU KNOW?

The Taíno once played a game almost like modern soccer. The remains of the playing courts, called *bateys,* have been found on Puerto Rico and other nearby islands.

landed at Puerto Rico. He named the island San Juan Bautista — Spanish for "St. John the Baptist." Columbus claimed the land as a colony for Spain. About thirty thousand Taíno lived in Puerto Rico when Columbus arrived.

Columbus did not stay in Puerto Rico, and the first Spanish settlers did not reach the island until 1508. Their leader, Juan Ponce de León, and the other settlers founded the town of Caparra, near San Juan Bay. Like most Spanish explorers, Ponce de León came looking for gold. The settlers forced the Taíno into slavery to mine the precious metal. Soon Puerto Rico was a major source of gold for the Spanish government. The Taíno rebelled in 1511, but the Spanish soldiers quickly restored order. By then, diseases from Europe had already killed many of the Taíno. Others fled high into the mountains or to neighboring islands. The Spaniards began to bring in African slaves to farm the sugarcane fields.

Spanish men often had children with their Taíno and African slaves. The children of Spanish and Native American heritage came to be called *mestizos*. Spaniards born in Puerto Rico or other West Indian colonies were called Creoles.

▼ Taíno Indians once played games and held religious ceremonies at this site in Ponce.

Colonial society was split into distinct social classes: slaves on the bottom, then mestizos, and then Spaniards and Creoles who controlled the economy and government.

The Spanish quickly mined all the gold in Puerto Rico. Spain's leaders then saw another role for Puerto Rico: It became an important base for the Spanish navy. By 1521, Spanish ships had a safe harbor in San Juan. The city had first been called Puerto Rico, or "rich port." By about 1530, the city was called San Juan and the entire island was called Puerto Rico. The Spanish built forts in San Juan, and troops and ships stationed there were used to defend other Spanish colonies in the West Indies. Puerto Rico was often the target of attacks by foreign raiders. In 1598, the English held San Juan for almost three months. In 1625, Dutch troops controlled part of Puerto Rico for almost a month.

Smugglers and Citizens

During most of the 1600s and 1700s, Spanish rulers did not pay much attention to Puerto Rico. Their only concern was getting money and resources from the island, and Puerto Ricans could trade only with Spain. This law forced some people to turn to smuggling to avoid taxes and get supplies they needed. By the middle of the eighteenth century,

▼ The Spanish used Taíno slaves to mine for gold.

Spanish leaders finally realized that their policies were hurting Puerto Rico. Alejandro O'Reilly, a Spanish official, visited the island in 1765. He noted that "In all the island, there are only two schools for children" and that many people "walk barefoot in the countryside." Spain sent new leaders and more money to Puerto Rico. It also allowed greater legal trade with other Caribbean islands, reducing smuggling. But at the same time, slavery increased, and the average Puerto Rican was still a poor, uneducated farmer.

By the early 1800s, Spain had lost its role as a major world power. Spanish colonists saw that they had a chance to win their independence, as the Americans had done in the American Revolution. Spain's rulers did not want a revolution in Puerto Rico. The Spanish let Puerto Ricans hold the first elections ever in 1809, allowing them to choose someone to represent them in Spain. Three years later, Puerto Ricans became Spanish citizens, and they slowly gained more legal rights. After 1823, however, Spain sent governors who ruled as dictators. Most Puerto Ricans still lived as poor farmers, known as *jíbaros*. Meanwhile, wealthy Spaniards and Creoles controlled the economy.

A New Colonial Ruler

During the nineteenth century, Puerto Ricans had mixed feelings about their relationship with Spain. Some wanted a democratic government while remaining tied to Spain. Others wanted complete independence. A doctor named Ramón Emeterio Betances was one of the main supporters of Puerto Rican independence. In 1864, he called for a revolution. Four years later, his supporters finally began their rebellion. They seized control of Lares, a town in the western part of the island. Carrying banners that declared "Liberty or Death," the rebels claimed Puerto Rico's independence. Spanish government troops came to the town, and within six weeks the revolution was over.

Juan Ponce de León

Juan Ponce de León was born about 1460 in Spain. He sailed with Christopher Columbus on his second voyage to the West Indies. A few years later, Ponce de León served as mayor of a Spanish settlement on the island of Hispaniola. During his time there, he amassed a large fortune. In 1508, he returned to Puerto Rico and founded the first Spanish settlement, serving as the first Spanish governor on the island. In 1513, Ponce de León left Puerto Rico with three ships and sailed to Florida, claiming the land for Spain. Once again, Ponce de León went looking for gold. Legends say that he also searched for a magical "fountain of youth," whose flowing water supposedly kept people young forever. He explored the waters around Florida before returning to Spain. Ponce de León eventually returned to Puerto Rico, and in 1521 he launched a second expedition to Florida. Trying to start a colony there, the explorer was wounded in a battle with Native Americans. He later died from the wound on the island of Cuba and his body was buried in Puerto Rico.

This failed revolution was known as *El Grito de Lares* — "the Shout of Lares." It remains a symbol of the Puerto Rican desire for independence.

As Puerto Ricans debated their status, some changes took place. Slavery was abolished in 1873, and in 1897, Spain granted Puerto Rico a large degree of independence. That freedom, however, did not last long.

In 1898, relations between Spain and the United States soured as the Spanish tried to end a rebellion in Cuba. After a U.S. naval ship exploded in Cuban waters, the United States declared war on Spain. On July 25, 1898, U.S. troops landed in Puerto Rico, quickly defeating the few Spanish troops on the island. When the war ended with a U.S. victory, the United States took control of Puerto Rico and several other Spanish colonies.

U.S. leaders saw Puerto Rico as a port for its navy and a cheap source of sugar and other crops. The United States made some improvements on the island, building schools, roads, and hospitals. Most Puerto Ricans, however, did not welcome their new rulers. The United States tried to introduce a new culture and a new language — English. U.S. businesses took over some Puerto Rican farms. Many

▼ The Spanish continued work on the El Morro Fortress through the eighteenth century. Today, the fort is famous for its guard houses, or *garitas*.

Americans refused to believe that Puerto Ricans could rule their island themselves.

Changing Relationship

In 1917, a law called the Jones Act made Puerto Ricans U.S. citizens, but they still lacked many rights and would elect only some of their leaders. The U.S. presence also had not helped the average Puerto Rican, who still earned just a few hundred dollars a year. Poverty increased during the Great Depression of the 1930s. Some Puerto Ricans once again began thinking about independence. The Nationalist Party, led by Pedro Albizu Campos, turned to violence to promote the call for independence. In 1937, nineteen people died during fighting in the city of Ponce.

Puerto Rico saw some improvement during the 1940s. In 1946, President Harry Truman appointed the first Puerto Rican native as governor. Two years later, Puerto Ricans elected their own governor for the first time. Their choice was Luis Muñoz Marín, who had worked for greater independence from the United States. Muñoz Marín backed the plan to give Puerto Rico a constitution and make it a commonwealth. He also supported Operation Bootstrap, a program that encouraged U.S. companies to build plants on the island. Puerto Ricans called Operation Bootstrap *Fomento*, which means "development." Under the plan, the number of factories in Puerto Rico rose from eighty-two in 1952 to more than seven hundred just ten years later. Operation Bootstrap provided more jobs for Puerto Ricans, but many still lacked work. During the 1950s, thousands of Puerto Ricans began leaving the island for the mainland.

Gradually, Operation Bootstrap helped make manufacturing the most important part of the Puerto Rican economy. Today, compared to other islands in the West Indies, Puerto Rico is wealthy. Compared to the fifty states, however, income is low. A special law once reduced taxes for U.S. companies on the island, but these tax breaks will end in 2006. Puerto Ricans are looking for new ways to keep their economy strong as they continue to wrestle with their relationship with the United States.

▲ This 1999 celebration marked the anniversary of the 1868 rebellion in Lares, fought to win Puerto Rico's independence from Spain. Some residents still seek independence for their island.

A Dangerous Position

Puerto Rico sits in the path of many hurricanes that hit the West Indies. Since 1508, more than seventy have hit the island. One storm in 1899 killed three thousand people. More recently, in 1998, Hurricane Georges destroyed 80,000 homes.

A Colorful Blend

> From the variety and mixture of peoples results
> an equivocal character difficult to explain . . .
>
> — *Friar Iñigo Abbad y Lasierra,*
> Historia Geográphica, Civil y Natural de
> San Juan de Bautista de Puerto Rico, *1788*

With a population of just over 3.8 million, Puerto Rico has more citizens than twenty-five U.S. states. The residents of Puerto Rico are crowded into a small area, giving the island a population density of 1,112 people per square mile (429 per sq km) — higher than any U.S. state and second only to the District of Columbia. From 1990 to 2000, Puerto Rico added slightly fewer than three hundred thousand people, a growth rate of 8.1 percent. Most Puerto Ricans — about 70 percent in 1990 — live in urban areas. Most major cities, such as San Juan, Ponce, Bayamón, and Carolina, are located near the coast. San Juan and the cities and towns near it have just over one-third of the island's residents.

Almost all Puerto Ricans are Hispanic. On the U.S. census, American Hispanics can classify themselves as

Age Distribution in Puerto Rico
(2000 Census)

Age	Population
0–4	295,406
5–19	924,398
20–24	301,191
25–44	1,049,995
45–64	812,483
65 & over	425,137

Across The Decades

Puerto Rico's three largest foreign-born groups for 1910 and 1990

	1910			1990	
Spain	France	St Thomas, Virgin Islands	Dominican Republic	Cuba	Spain
6,630	681	560	37,505	19,736	4,579

Total island population: 1,118,012
Total foreign-born: 11,776 (1.1%)

Total island population: 3,522,037
Total foreign-born: 90,713 (2.6%)

Patterns of Immigration

In 1998, the total number of people who immigrated to Puerto Rico was 3,251. Of that number, the largest immigrant groups were from the Dominican Republic (81.4%), Cuba (4.5%), and Colombia (2.2%)

belonging to any race or report being a mix of races. Just over 80 percent of Puerto Rican Hispanics classify themselves as white, while 8 percent say they are black. Asians, Native Americans, and Pacific Islanders make up just a small part of the island's population. Historically, members of different races and ethnic groups in Puerto Rico have married each other, creating a wide mix of racial and cultural backgrounds. This mix has limited racism: blacks, whites, and people of mixed backgrounds easily live side by side in Puerto Rico. In the past, however, African slaves and their descendants did face some prejudice.

Although most Puerto Ricans call themselves Hispanic, the Spanish were not the only Europeans to settle on the island. Some people can trace their roots to settlers from France, Great Britain, and Germany, as well as from Spaniards who first lived in other parts of the New World before reaching Puerto Rico. After 1898, Americans of different ethnic and racial backgrounds also came to the island. All these different settlers added to the ethnic mix that shapes the people of the island today.

▲ Fancy costumes and dancing play a large part in many Puerto Rican festivals.

DID YOU KNOW?

Santos, wooden statues of Catholic saints, are also important to some followers of Santeria and spiritualism. The statues are valued today by museums and art collectors as important expressions of folk art.

Heritage and Background, Puerto Rico — Year 2000

▶ Here is a look at the racial backgrounds of Puerto Ricans today.

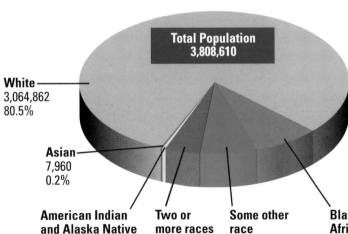

Total Population 3,808,610

White
3,064,862
80.5%

Asian
7,960
0.2%

Hawaiian or other Pacific Islander
1,093
0.03%

American Indian and Alaska Native
13,336
0.4%

Two or more races
158,415
4.2%

Some other race
260,011
6.8%

Black or African American
302,933
8.0%

Note: 98.8% (3,762,746) of the population identify themselves as **Hispanic** or **Latino,** a cultural designation that crosses racial lines. Hispanics and Latinos are counted in this category as well as the racial category of their choice.

Languages

Spanish and English are the official languages in Puerto Rico. About 25 percent of the people are fluent in both languages. English is most common in large cities, as compared to smaller towns and villages.

The language of Puerto Rico's Taíno also endures on the island. Taíno words are used for cities and towns, such as Caguas, Bayamón, and Guánica. Some Spanish and English words are based on such Taíno words as *hamaca* ("hammock") and *barbacoa* ("barbecue").

Religion

Traditions from three continents shape most of the religious life on Puerto Rico. The Taíno religion featured many gods, with the goddess Atabey considered the greatest of them all. Today some Taíno still follow their traditional religion.

Educational Levels of Puerto Rico Workers (age 25 and over)	
Less than 9th grade	581,225
9th to 12th grade, no diploma	335,179
High school graduate, including equivalency	509,856
Some college, no degree or associate degree	443,813
Bachelor's degree	310,443
Graduate or professional degree	107,810

▼ Swimmers enjoy the warm waters of the Atlantic Ocean with the skyline of San Juan, Puerto Rico's largest city and capital, silhouetted in the sunset.

The Spanish brought Roman Catholicism to the island, and its churches and leaders play an important role in Puerto Rican life. People celebrate the feasts of Catholic saints and many have *santos* — wooden statues that represent the saints. The Catholicism in Puerto Rico blended with Taíno beliefs and the religions brought by African slaves. In some of these African religions, people worshiped spirits believed to live in nature. Drumming and dancing were important parts of their religious ceremonies. Today, some people practice Santeria, a religion developed by African slaves who were taken to the Caribbean. The slaves worshiped Catholic saints while keeping many of their old religious beliefs. Cuban immigrants brought Santeria to the island. Some Puerto Ricans also believe in spiritualism, in which the spirits of dead people exist on Earth. The belief in spirits also influences some followers of other religions on the island.

Although Catholicism and traditional religions are most common, other faiths are also represented in Puerto Rico. After 1898, Protestant missionaries came to the island from the United States. Today, Protestant churches in Puerto Rico include Methodist and Pentecostal. By some accounts, Protestants make up about one-fourth of the island's population. There is also a small Jewish community.

Education

Under Spanish rule, the first schools in Puerto Rico were run by the Catholic Church. Later, the Spanish government promoted the building of schools, with religious instruction still important. Soon after the Americans came to Puerto Rico, they began building public schools that did not stress religious teachings. Today, all children between the ages of six and seventeen are required to attend school, public or private. Classes are taught in Spanish and students study English throughout elementary and secondary school. About 90 percent of Puerto Ricans are literate.

The major university on the island is the University of Puerto Rico, with its main campus at Rio Piedras in San Juan. Other colleges include the Inter American University, Caribbean University, and Polytechnic University of Puerto Rico. A high percentage of Puerto Rico's college-age students attend some kind of university or college.

▲ A procession of Catholic children winds its way to the San Andres church in Barranquitas. Colorful celebrations like this are an important part of religious life in Puerto Rico.

Taíno Culture Today

Today, some people, both in Puerto Rico and in the United States, are descendants of the Taíno. Members of the Jatibonicu tribe live in the mountains of central Puerto Rico as well as on the mainland. They are known as the "Great People of the Sacred High Waters." Tribal members preserve ancient religious beliefs and games while drawing attention to the history of the Taíno in Puerto Rico.

Tropical Paradise

> The land of Borinquen, where I was born,
> is a flowering garden of magical beauty.
> — *"La Borinqueña," the Puerto Rican anthem*

If Puerto Rico were a state, it would rank as the third smallest — only Rhode Island and Delaware are smaller. The island's land area is 3,425 square miles (8,871 sq km). The territory of Puerto Rico includes several smaller islands. The most important are Vieques and Culebra on the east coast and Mona on the west coast. Puerto Rico is part of a group of islands called the Greater Antilles. These islands and two other groups of islands form the West Indies. Puerto Rico's closest neighbors are the island of Hispaniola to the west and the U.S. Virgin Islands to the east. Puerto Rico is about 1,000 miles (1,609 km) southeast of Florida. Close to the island is the Puerto Rico Trench, the deepest spot in the Atlantic Ocean, which plunges more than 27,000 feet (8,200 m) under the surface of the water.

The Mountains

Most of Puerto Rico is covered with hills and mountains, except along the coasts. Many of the hills are farmed. The largest mountain range, the Cordillera Central, is in the

Highest Point

Cerro de Punto
4,390 feet (1,338 m)
above sea level

DID YOU KNOW?

Just southeast of Ponce is Caja de Muertos Island. The name means "dead man's coffin." From the mainland, the island looks somewhat like a coffin floating on the water.

▼ A manatee; palm trees on a Caribbean beach; Arecibo Observatory; a waterfall in El Yunque; the courtyard of San Cristobal; a scarlet macaw.

south-central part of the island. The range runs from east to west for about 60 miles (97 km). The tallest peak in the Cordillera Central — and on the island — is Cerro de Punto. Puerto Rico's rivers are small, with the largest of them starting in the Cordillera Central and flowing north to the Atlantic Ocean.

Puerto Rico's other notable mountain range is the Sierra de Luquillo, located in the island's northeast corner. El Toro, located in the El Yunque rain forest, is the tallest mountain in the range, at 3,533 feet (1,077 m). Between the major two mountain ranges is the Turabo Valley, a farming region.

The Coastal Lowlands

Flat stretches of land lie along the north and south coasts of Puerto Rico. The northern lowlands feature a large percentage of the island's population and major industry. The southern coast tends to be drier than the north. Some crops are grown along all the coasts of the island.

In the northwest region, close to the foothills, lies the karst country. Karst describes land marked with small hills and sinkholes, with caves and tunnels underneath them. Limestone rock is worn away by rain, creating this unique landscape. Arecibo is in the center of Puerto Rico's karst country, and the Arecibo Observatory sits in a large sinkhole. The region is also home to the Rio Camuy cave park.

Plants and Animals

For a small island, Puerto Rico has a wide assortment of wildlife. Some of the plants and animals have been on the island for thousands of years. Others were brought by the Spanish and the Americans. Tropical rain forests and other forests cover the mountains and hills in the northern and central regions, while the south has plants adapted to its

Average January temperature
San Juan: 76°F (24°C)
Santa Isabel: 72°F (22°C)

Average July temperature
San Juan: 81°F (27°C)
Santa Isabel: 80°F (27°C)

Average yearly rainfall
San Juan: 59 inches (150 cm)
Santa Isabel: 33 inches (84 cm)

DID YOU KNOW?

The El Yunque Rain Forest has more than 240 kinds of trees. About 88 of these species of trees are found only at El Yunque.

Largest Lakes

La Plata
1,211 acres (490 hectares)

Guajataca
581 acres (235 ha)

Carraizo (Loiza)
566 acres (229 ha)

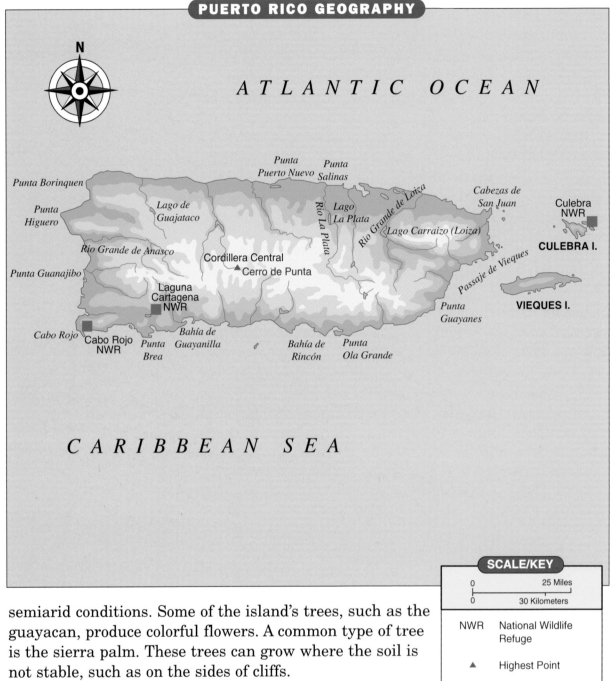

ATLANTIC OCEAN

Punta Borinquen

Punta
Higuero

Punta
Puerto Nuevo

Punta
Salinas

Cabezas de
San Juan

Culebra
NWR

CULEBRA I.

Lago de
Guajataco

Lago
La Plata

Rio La Plata

Rio Grande de Loiza

Lago Carraizo (Loiza)

Rio Grande de Anasco

Cordillera Central
Cerro de Punta

Punta Guanajibo

Laguna
Cartagena
NWR

Passaje de Vieques

VIEQUES I.

Punta
Guayanes

Cabo Rojo
Cabo Rojo
NWR

Punta
Brea

Bahía de
Guayanilla

Bahía de
Rincón

Punta
Ola Grande

CARIBBEAN SEA

SCALE/KEY

0   25 Miles

0   30 Kilometers

NWR   National Wildlife
Refuge

▲   Highest Point

▦   Mountains

semiarid conditions. Some of the island's trees, such as the guayacan, produce colorful flowers. A common type of tree is the sierra palm. These trees can grow where the soil is not stable, such as on the sides of cliffs.

Tropical trees, like the ones found on Puerto Rico, produce hardwood useful in constructing buildings and making furniture. Most of the island's forests were cut down over the centuries. During the twentieth century, islanders began replanting forests, and the U.S. government preserved some existing forests so their trees could not be cut. El Yunque in the northeast and Toro Negro in the south are two of these protected areas.

Puerto Rico has a wide assortment of animals, from

the common to the rare. The Spanish brought horses and cattle to the island. Rats also found their way ashore from Spanish ships. A later arrival was the mongoose, brought to the island to kill rats that were destroying sugarcane. Puerto Rico has several hundred types of birds, including hummingbirds, doves, owls, and pigeons. Waterbirds, such as herons and pelicans, are found along the coasts. Reptiles and amphibians include a wide assortment of lizards and the beloved coquí tree frog. A variety of sea creatures, from fish and shellfish to sea horses and coral, live in the waters off Puerto Rico. Many types of sharks swim in the warm island waters.

The national government tries to preserve forests and has set aside land as wildlife preserves. The Cabo Rojo National Wildlife Refuge is on Puerto Rico's west coast, and the island of Culebra has a similar refuge. Cabo Rojo is the home to the yellow-shouldered blackbird, one of several endangered species on the island. At Culebra, leatherbacks and other large sea turtles nest on the beaches. The leatherback is another endangered species, as is the rare Puerto Rican parrot, a colorful bird found only in El Yunque.

Major Rivers	
Rio La Plata	46 miles (74 km)
Rio Grande de Añasco	40 miles (64 km)
Rio Grande de Loíza	40 miles (64 km)

▼ Puerto Rico's natural beauty is sometimes destroyed by tropical storms, as shown after Hurricane Georges hit the island in 1998.

Building a Better Future

> The people of Puerto Rico want to work.
> — *Governor Sila Calderon, 2001*

Puerto Rico has been called the success story of the Caribbean. It has the highest income in the region. Many highly skilled, well-educated Puerto Ricans have good jobs in manufacturing, construction, and high-technology fields. Yet compared to the United States, poverty is still high, and many people who want jobs cannot find them. Both the U.S. and Puerto Rican governments are trying to tap the skills of the island's residents and end the history of poverty in remote areas.

Wealth from the Land

The Spanish introduced sugarcane, coffee, and tobacco farming to Puerto Rico. They also brought tropical fruits, such as pineapples. Agriculture remained the most important part of Puerto Rico's economy until the 1950s. Since then, farming has declined as the major source of wealth on the island, but Puerto Ricans still raise crops and animals for food.

The most important agricultural activity is raising livestock: cattle, chickens, and pigs. The cattle provide both meat and milk, and dairy products are the top source of farm income. Next come chickens and eggs. The most valuable crops are coffee, fruits, and ornamental plants — plants used decoratively in landscaping or inside buildings. Sugarcane, once the major crop on the island, now contributes only a small amount to Puerto Rico's economy.

Puerto Rico has limited natural resources that can be tapped to provide jobs and income. Most trees on the island were cut before 1900. Much of the replanting since then has been in protected areas where logging is not allowed.

Top Employers (of workers age sixteen and over)
Services 38.0%
Wholesale and retail trade 16.1%
Federal, state, and local government (including military) 10.7%
Construction 8.6%
Manufacturing ... 13.5%
Finance, insurance, and real estate ... 5.0%
Transportation, communications, and utilities 6.4%
Agriculture, forestry, and fisheries 1.7%

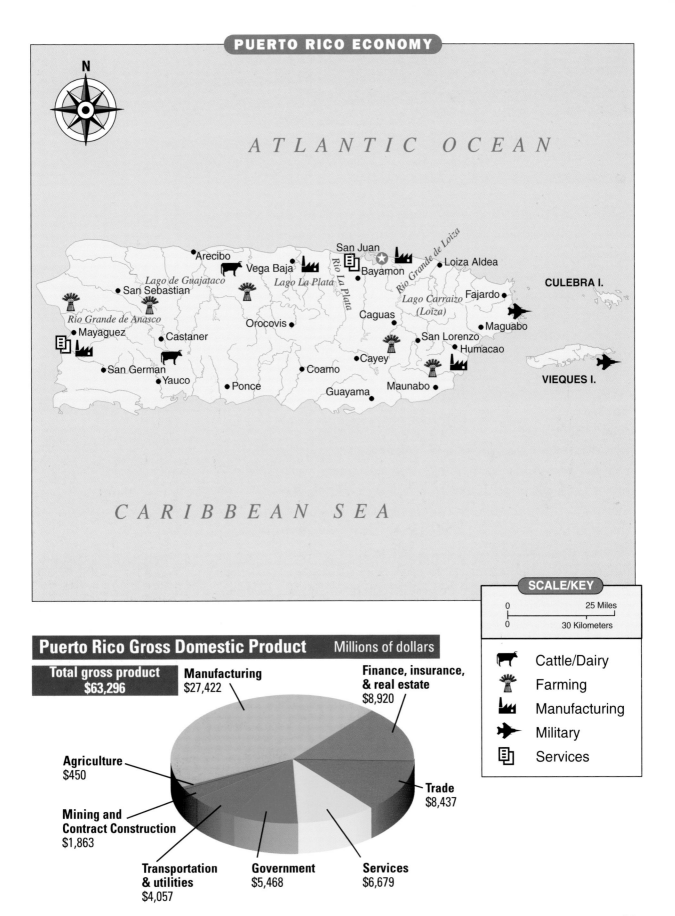

N

ATLANTIC OCEAN

Arecibo
Vega Baja
San Juan
Bayamon
Loiza Aldea
Lago de Guajataco
San Sebastian
Lago La Plata
Rio Grande de Loiza
CULEBRA I.
Fajardo
Rio Grande de Anasco
Lago Carraizo (Loiza)
Orocovis
Caguas
Mayaguez
Castaner
Maguabo
San Lorenzo
Humacao
San German
Cayey
Yauco
Coamo
Ponce
Guayama
Maunabo
VIEQUES I.
Rio La Plata

CARIBBEAN SEA

SCALE/KEY

0 — 25 Miles
0 — 30 Kilometers

Cattle/Dairy
Farming
Manufacturing
Military
Services

Puerto Rico Gross Domestic Product
Millions of dollars

Total gross product
$63,296

Manufacturing
$27,422

Finance, insurance, & real estate
$8,920

Agriculture
$450

Trade
$8,437

Mining and Contract Construction
$1,863

Transportation & utilities
$4,057

Government
$5,468

Services
$6,679

Mining in Puerto Rico centers on sand, gravel, and stone, which are used for construction. The island has small amounts of gold and other precious metals, but concerns for the environment have limited mining them. Fishing is only a small part of the local economy. Some tourists catch fish for fun, but commercial fishing is not important. Several companies built plants to can tuna, but production and jobs have been cut in recent years. The companies have moved their plants to countries where they can pay workers less money.

Manufacturing

Operation Bootstrap and U.S. tax laws turned Puerto Rico from an island of farmers into a major manufacturing center. At first, manufacturers made goods such as ceramics, clothes, and shoes. Over time, however, the chemical industry became the major source of manufacturing jobs. Puerto Rico is the world's top producer of pharmaceuticals and other health-care products, with more than one hundred drug companies represented there. Another important industry is the manufacturing of electronics. Electronic goods include instruments used in scientific research and parts for computers. Clothing manufacturing, although less important than it was during the 1950s and 1960s, still plays a key role in the economy. The clothing industry is the third largest source of manufacturing jobs on the island.

In recent years, small companies have been playing a larger role in the Puerto Rican economy. Many of these businesses are involved in printing, publishing, and furniture making.

Services and Tourism

The service industry can be broadly defined to include government services, retail, finances, health, education, and

▲ Coffee plantations like these dot many Puerto Rican hillsides. Some coffee is also grown near tropical forests.

Going Organic

Most of the large farms that remain on Puerto Rico focus on growing one crop and rely on chemicals to kill damaging insects and weeds. A small number of farmers, however, are trying to bring organic farming to the island. The University of Puerto Rico recently began offering a degree in sustainable farming, which stresses growing crops without the use of chemicals. This new movement also encourages growing a wide range of crops on individual farms.

social welfare. The U.S. and the commonwealth governments are among the largest employers in Puerto Rico. The U.S. military has a number of bases on the island, including a navy base and a training center for the national guard. Puerto Rico's financial center is in San Juan, in a district known as Hato Rey. The tourism industry adds more than $2 billion each year to Puerto Rico's economy. Tourists enjoy the island's fine beaches and explore its natural wonders.

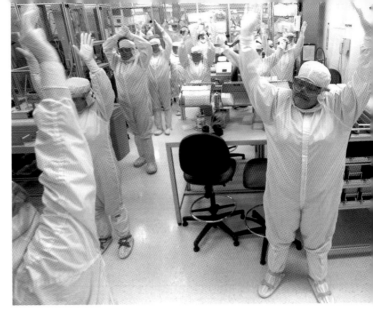

▲ These workers in a San Germán drug company take an exercise break during the day.

Transportation and Communication

Puerto Rico relies on planes and ships to transport goods and people to the island. San Juan, Ponce, and Mayagüez are the major ports, and each of those cities also has an airport. Small planes fly between the island's airports, but most Puerto Ricans travel by car. The island has 146 vehicles per square mile (56 per sq km) — one of the highest densities of vehicles in the world. Residents also rely on bus service and *publicos* — private cars or minivans used as taxis. Vehicles on the island travel on more than 14,000 miles (22,500 km) of roads. Most of them are paved, but dirt roads are still used in some small communities.

For communications, Puerto Ricans can choose from more than one hundred radio stations and twenty television stations. They also have access to U.S. broadcasts through cable and satellite TV. A modern phone service links the island to the United States by both satellite and underwater cables. The island has a variety of weekly newspapers and several daily ones, including *El Nuevo Día* and the *San Juan Star*.

For years, the only railroad on Puerto Rico was a small stretch of track used to haul sugarcane to port. Now, Puerto Rico has its first passenger train service, the Tren Urbano. First tested in 2000, the train is designed for commuters. It connects San Juan with nearby cities and towns.

Major Airport		
Airport	**Location**	**Passengers per year (2000)**
Luis Muñoz Marín International	San Juan	9,978,146

Governing a Commonwealth

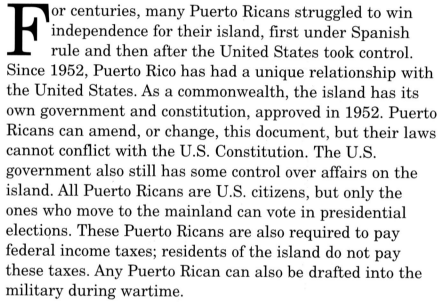

> As we see it, Puerto Rico is a new kind of state, both in the sense of the United States federal system and in the general sense of a people organized to govern themselves.
>
> — *Luis Muñoz Marín, 1959*

For centuries, many Puerto Ricans struggled to win independence for their island, first under Spanish rule and then after the United States took control. Since 1952, Puerto Rico has had a unique relationship with the United States. As a commonwealth, the island has its own government and constitution, approved in 1952. Puerto Ricans can amend, or change, this document, but their laws cannot conflict with the U.S. Constitution. The U.S. government also still has some control over affairs on the island. All Puerto Ricans are U.S. citizens, but only the ones who move to the mainland can vote in presidential elections. These Puerto Ricans are also required to pay federal income taxes; residents of the island do not pay these taxes. Any Puerto Rican can also be drafted into the military during wartime.

Like the U.S. government, the Puerto Rican government is divided into three branches: executive, legislative, and judicial. The executive branch carries out the laws, the legislative branch makes laws, and the judicial branch interprets the laws and how they are carried out.

The Executive Branch

The governor of Puerto Rico is the leader of the executive branch. This branch carries out the laws passed by the legislature. The governor appoints all judges and the members of the cabinet. The cabinet members lead different executive departments and advise the governor. The Puerto Rican senate must approve the governor's choices for these positions. The governor also accepts or rejects laws passed by the legislative branch. During an emergency, the

Commonwealth Constitution

We, the people of Puerto Rico, in order to organize ourselves politically on a fully democratic basis, to promote the general welfare, and to secure for ourselves and our posterity the complete enjoyment of human rights, placing our trust in Almighty God, do ordain and establish this Constitution for the commonwealth which, in the exercise of our natural rights, we now create within our union with the United States of America.

— *Preamble to the Commonwealth of Puerto Rico Constitution*

Elected Posts in the Executive Branch		
Office	Length of Term	Term Limits
Governor	4 years	none

governor can declare martial law, putting the military in control of the island.

Second in power to the governor is the secretary of state. The person holding this executive position serves as governor when the actual governor leaves the island and takes over the position if the governor resigns or dies in office.

The Legislative Branch

The Puerto Rico legislature has two houses, or branches — the house of representatives and the senate. Voters choose representatives every four years. The house has fifty-one members. One is chosen for each of Puerto Rico's forty house districts, and eleven are chosen from the island at large. The senate has twenty-seven members, with voters electing two in each of eight senatorial districts and eleven at large. Two extra seats can be added to either house if one party has too many members. These extra seats go to other parties with fewer elected members.

The Judicial Branch

Puerto Rico's judicial branch has a variety of courts, with judges appointed by the governor and confirmed by the senate. The highest court is the supreme court. It has six associate justices, and a chief justice. All members serve for life. The supreme court reviews decisions made by lower courts and decides if the decisions fairly apply the Commonwealth's constitution.

Puerto Rico's other courts include the courts of appeals,

▼ El Capitolio, the capitol in Puerto Rico, opened in 1929.

superior courts, district courts, and municipal courts. Unlike the supreme court justices, the judges on these courts serve limited terms, ranging from five to sixteen years.

When federal laws are broken, trials are held in the U.S. District Court in San Juan. The seven judges on this court are appointed by the president of the United States. Court cases that are heard by the Puerto Rico Supreme Court can be appealed to another U.S. district court, based on the mainland.

Local Government
Each state has a number of different local governments that handle such issues as local education, maintaining roads and public spaces, collecting some taxes, and enforcing local and state laws. Puerto Rico has seventy-eight local political units called *municipos*, or municipalities. Some are cities, while others include a large town and surrounding villages. Voters in each *municipo* elect a mayor and an assembly. The assembly is the legislative branch and the mayor is the executive for the municipalities.

National Representation
Puerto Rican voters send one representative, called a resident commissioner, to the U.S. House of Representatives. This position was created by a U.S. law in 1900. No one from Puerto Rico represents the island in the U.S. Senate. The resident commissioner can speak on issues debated in the House and serves on the committees that draft bills, but cannot vote on the final passage of bills.

Political Parties and the Status Issue
Puerto Rico has three main political parties. Each one has a strong position on what kind of relationship the island should have with the United States. This question of Puerto Rico's status dominates much of the political debate on the island.

Legislature			
House	**Number of Members**	**Length of Term**	**Term Limits**
Senate	27* senators	4 years	none
House of Representatives	51* representatives	4 years	none
*Two extra members can be added as needed to prevent one party from having more than two-thirds of the members.			

The Popular Democratic Party (PDP) has been the most successful party in Puerto Rico since 1940. This party wants to keep Puerto Rico a commonwealth. The major challenge to the PDP comes from the New Progressive Party, which supports statehood for the island. The smaller Puerto Rico Independence Party wants the island to be an independent nation. Several other minor parties take part in the island's politics.

In 1998, Puerto Ricans had the chance to vote on the status issue — the third time since 1952. A slight majority of voters selected "none of the above" over statehood, commonwealth status, or independence. Statehood was a close second. The results meant that Puerto Rico kept its current status. The PDP advised its members to vote for "none of the above" as a protest. It opposed the wording used on the ballot, which had been written by the New Progressive Party.

▶ Supporters of statehood for Puerto Rico hold up a sign saying "Statehood Now" and a U.S. flag during a rally.

Island Fun

> I consumed my joy from the countryside,
> and I'm as happy as the day,
> just like the industrious honey bee,
> and as radiant as the sun.
>
> — *Virgilio Dávila, from the poem* "The Jibaro"

Puerto Ricans love to celebrate their rich culture, shaped by the blending of European, African, and Native American lifestyles. Puerto Rico has been part of the United States for more than one hundred years, but the Spanish language and culture still dominate the island. Taíno culture remains in words, food, and art. The African slaves who were brought to Puerto Rico influenced the island's music. Puerto Ricans are proud of this unique heritage.

Art and Museums

Puerto Rican art goes back to the Taíno and other early Native Americans. The Taíno were expert woodworkers, and their carved items included thrones for their rulers. The Taíno also left behind petroglyphs, or rock carvings, that showed images of their gods and the spirits that lived in nature.

When the Spanish arrived, they brought their styles of architecture and art. In Old San Juan, buildings painted with pastel colors line narrow cobblestone streets, similar to the architecture of the period in southern Spain. Formal arts, such as painting, did not develop until the eighteenth century. The first great Puerto Rican painter was José

▼ Clara Cave, at Rio Camuy Cave Park, is almost 700 feet (213 m) long.

▲ These petroglyphs
at Caguana Indian
Ceremonial Park
show examples of
Taíno art.

Campeche. The son of a freed slave, Campeche painted in the style of the European masters of the day, learning his craft by studying their works. Another great artist on the island was Francisco Oller. He was influenced by the Impressionists, French painters of the late nineteenth century. Many of Oller's works showed the scenery of Puerto Rico.

Taíno art, works by Puerto Ricans, and paintings from around the world can be found in Puerto Rico's many museums. San Juan has more than a dozen museums, including the Institute of Puerto Rican Culture. A new art museum opened in Santurce, just outside San Juan, in 2000. The island's most famous art museum is in Ponce. Located in a modern building with six-sided rooms, the museum has almost two thousand works of art.

Puerto Rico also has a long tradition of folk art. Along with the religious statues called santos, island craftspeople create colorful masks called *vejigantes* out of papier-mâché that are worn during festivals.

Music and Literature

Making music is almost a way of life in Puerto Rico. The first Spanish sailors sang folk songs and ballads, and African slaves brought the rhythmic dances of their homelands. Over the centuries, Puerto Ricans developed a number of musical

Art Today

Besides José Campeche and Francisco Oller, the most famous Puerto Rican artists, the island has produced many other talented painters and sculptors. These include Rafael Ferrer, who left the island and now paints in New York, and Myrna Baez, an artist who both paints and sculpts.

styles and dances that have spread around the world.

Several instruments were developed on the island. The Taíno used gourds to make guiros and maracas. Guiros have ridges that are scraped with a stick, while maracas, with dried seeds rattling inside, are shaken in time to the music. Africans brought drums and used them in a dance style known as *bomba*. Another musical style in Puerto Rico is *plena*, which also features drums and other handheld percussion instruments.

A more modern form of Puerto Rican music is salsa, which combines the island's percussion instruments with the sounds of jazz. This up-tempo music is perfect for fast dances. Tito Puente, the son of Puerto Ricans who moved to New York, is sometimes called the "king of salsa."

Classical music has also thrived in Puerto Rico. The island has a symphony orchestra and a ballet company. During the twentieth century, world-famous cellist Pablo Casals, a Spaniard, moved to Puerto Rico and helped spark a deeper interest in classical music.

Puerto Rican writing started with the arrival of the Spanish, as Juan Ponce de León and other early settlers

▲ Musicians play distinctive Puerto Rican music to entertain tourists and natives alike in old San Juan.

A Cultural Symbol

Since Manuel Alonso published *El Gíbaro*, peasant farmers called *jíbaros* have been featured in many Puerto Rican stories and poems. They represent the strength, pride, and independence of the Puerto Rican people.

recorded their observations of the island. Fiction and poetry developed more slowly, but by the mid-nineteenth century the island had a strong literary tradition. One of the first classics was *El Gíbaro*, by Manuel Alonso, published in 1849. The book has poems, stories, and essays about the *jibaros,* peasants who lived in the mountains. The island has also produced a number of fine poets, such as José Gautier Benítez, Luis Muñoz Rivera, and Julia de Burgos.

Sports

Puerto Rico fields its own teams during the Olympics, and Puerto Rican athletes often play on professional U.S. teams. Baseball and basketball are two popular team sports, along with soccer. The island has a winter baseball league that features U.S. stars, and semiprofessional basketball teams compete across the island. Most high schools have soccer teams, and a few private schools also play American football.

Puerto Ricans also enjoy individual sports. The island has produced several world champions in boxing. Outdoor activities include tennis, golf, and horse racing. Not surprisingly, water sports, including surfing, boating, and fishing, are also popular on the island.

▼ Built in 1882, Ponce's Parque de Bombas firehouse is now a museum.

Important Puerto Ricans

Our people is an heroic people. Our people is courageous.
— *Pedro Albizu Campo, quoted by Stan Steiner in*
The Islands: The Worlds of the Puerto Ricans, 1974

Following are only a few of the thousands of people who were born, died, or spent much of their lives in Puerto Rico and made extraordinary contributions to the commonwealth and the nation.

RAMÓN POWER Y GIRALT
POLITICIAN

BORN: *October 21, 1775, San Juan*
DIED: *June 10, 1813, Cadiz, Spain*

The son of a wealthy family, Ramón Power y Giralt won the first election ever held in Puerto Rico. He attended schools in Spain and France, and served in the Spanish navy before starting his political career. In January, 1809, Spain let Puerto Ricans elect their first representative to the Cortes, the Spanish legislative assembly. This event gave Puerto Ricans their own voice in government. Power y Giralt beat out fourteen other men to win the seat. He actually had to win a second election, held the next year, before the government allowed him to enter the assembly. Once a member of the assembly, he was then elected its vice president. Power y Giralt helped pass laws that gave Puerto Rico more freedom to run its own affairs. His home, in Old San Juan, has been restored and is the office building for the Puerto Rico Conservation Trust.

RAMÓN EMETERIO BETANCES
DOCTOR AND POLITICIAN

BORN: *April 8, 1827, Cabo Rojo*
DIED: *September 18, 1898, Nevilly, France*

Rámon Betances studied medicine in France, then returned to his homeland in 1855. He set up a hospital in Mayagüez to treat victims of a cholera epidemic that swept the island. Betances also took time from medicine to write about the political situation in Puerto Rico. His strong views on independence and abolishing slavery led the Spanish government to force him off the island several times. Living in New York and Santo Domingo, he urged Puerto Ricans to use violence, if necessary, to achieve independence. After the failed revolution of 1868, which he inspired, Betances moved to France.

JOSÉ DE DIEGO
POET AND POLITICIAN

BORN: *April 16, 1866, Aguadilla*
DIED: *July 17, 1921, New York, NY*

Like Luis Muñoz Rivera, another well-known poet and politician of his era, José de Diego wanted independence for Puerto Rico. One of his dreams was the creation of a union of Caribbean islands with Spanish-speaking residents. Diego founded the Autonomist Party, which struggled for greater freedom from Spain. In 1904, he and Rivera started the Unionist Party, another political party that sought independence, this time from the United States. Diego held several positions in the Puerto Rican government between 1897 and 1918. He served as president of the House of Delegates from 1907-1917 and speaker of the House of Representatives from 1917-1918. He also published several books of poetry and died while giving a recital of his poems. In death, Diego is thought of as the founder of modern poetry movement in Puerto Rico. He was thought to be a brilliant speaker in both government and creative circles.

PABLO CASALS
CLASSICAL MUSICIAN

BORN: *December 29, 1876, Vendrell, Catalonia, Spain*
DIED: *October 22, 1973, San Juan*

As a young boy, Pablo Casals studied violin, and he could also play piano, flute, and organ. Today he is remembered as one of the greatest cellists of all time. He gave concerts around the world, recorded many albums, and was a conductor and composer as well as a musician. Casals was already a master of the cello when he moved to Puerto Rico in 1956. Both his mother and his wife had been born on the island. Casals founded a classical music festival and helped start the Puerto Rico Symphony Orchestra and a music school. A museum in Old San Juan is dedicated to his life and music.

PEDRO ALBIZU CAMPOS
POLITICIAN

BORN: *September 12, 1891, Tenerias*
DIED: *April 21, 1965, Hato Rey*

Orphaned as a boy, Pedro Albizu Campos won a scholarship to study in the United States and eventually earned two degrees from Harvard University. He also fought for the U.S. military during World War I. Returning to Puerto Rico, Albizu Campos became active in politics and was chosen head of the Nationalist Party in 1930. The Nationalists wanted independence at any cost — including violence. Albizu Campos was accused of trying to overthrow the U.S. government and spent several years in jail. Some Americans considered Albizu Campos a terrorist; Puerto Ricans who wanted independence considered him a hero.

FELISA RINCÓN DE GAUTIER
POLITICIAN

BORN: *January 9, 1897, Ceiba*
DIED: *September 16, 1994, San Juan*

A supporter of Puerto Rican independence, Felisa Rincón de Gautier entered politics during the 1930s. She helped form the Popular Democratic Party, which is still Puerto Rico's major party. In 1946, Rincón de Gautier became the first woman elected mayor of San Juan, and she held that position for twenty-two years. During the 1950s, she won fame for bringing plane-loads of snow to the city so local children could have snowball fights.

LUIS MUÑOZ MARÍN
GOVERNOR

BORN: *February 18, 1898, San Juan*
DIED: *April 30, 1980, San Juan*

Like his father Luis Muñoz Rivera, Luis Muñoz Marín became both a journalist and a politician. When he helped start the Popular Democratic Party, Muñoz Marín supported Puerto Rican independence. Later in his career, however, he strongly backed commonwealth status for the island. Muñoz Marín served as the first elected governor of Puerto Rico, holding office from 1949 to 1965. In 1963, he received the U.S. Presidential Medal of Freedom.

LUIS PALÉS MATOS
POET

BORN: *March 20, 1898, Guayama*
DIED: *February 23, 1959, San Juan*

Luis Palés Matos, considered one of the best Afro-Antillean poets, examined the lives and concerns of the descendants of African slaves brought to the Antilles. He published his first book of poetry while still a teenager. His books of poetry include *Tuntún de Pasa y Grifería*. Some people consider Palés Matos the greatest Puerto Rican poet of the twentieth century.

HORACIO RIVERO
U.S. ADMIRAL

BORN: *May 6, 1910, Ponce*
DIED: *September 24, 2000, San Diego, CA*

Horacio Rivero was the first Hispanic American to become a four-star officer in the U.S. military. Rivero was a four-star admiral in the U.S. Navy. Rivero moved from Puerto Rico to the mainland to attend the U.S. Naval Academy, graduating in 1931. During World War II, he served on several ships in the Pacific Ocean, earning two medals for his leadership. During the 1950s, he commanded two ships and held important positions in Washington, D.C. He was named a rear admiral in 1955 and received his four-star rank in 1964. After leaving the military in 1972, Rivero served as U.S. ambassador to Spain for three years.

JULIA DE BURGOS
POET

BORN: *February 17, 1917, Carolina*
DIED: *July 6, 1953, New York, NY*

Julia de Burgos wrote poetry on a wide range of topics, from love to politics. Her work was influenced by Pablo Neruda, a Chilean poet and political activist. A member of a group of writers based in San Juan, she published her first collection of poems in 1937. Her third book won a prize from the Institute of Puerto Rican Literature. In 1940, de Burgos left Puerto Rico for New York, where she wrote both poetry and essays on political issues. De Burgos was proud of her African heritage, and she tackled the issue of sexual equality long before most people of her generation.

RITA MORENO

ENTERTAINER

BORN: *December 11, 1931, Humacao*

Born Rosita Dolores Alverio, Rita Moreno has excelled as a singer, dancer, and actor. She first appeared on Broadway when she was thirteen and began acting in films the next year.

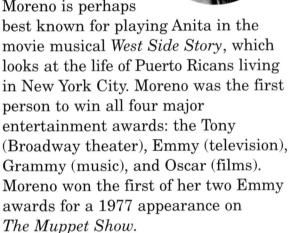

Moreno is perhaps best known for playing Anita in the movie musical *West Side Story*, which looks at the life of Puerto Ricans living in New York City. Moreno was the first person to win all four major entertainment awards: the Tony (Broadway theater), Emmy (television), Grammy (music), and Oscar (films). Moreno won the first of her two Emmy awards for a 1977 appearance on *The Muppet Show*.

ROBERTO CLEMENTE

BASEBALL PLAYER

BORN: *August 18, 1934, Carolina*
DIED: *December 31, 1972, between San Juan and Nicaragua*

To Puerto Ricans, Roberto Clemente is both a great athlete and a national hero. Clemente played outfield for the Pittsburgh Pirates from 1955 to 1972. During his career, he led the National League in hitting four times and won twelve Gold Gloves for his fielding. He was named the league's Most Valuable Player in 1966 and was the MVP of the 1971 World Series. In the last game of the 1972 season, Clemente smacked his three thousandth career hit — a milestone only the greatest hitters reach. That winter, Clemente died in a plane crash while taking aid to earthquake victims in Nicaragua. In 1973, in honor of his work on and off the ball field, he became the first Puerto Rican named to the National Baseball Hall of Fame.

ANTONIA NOVELLO

DOCTOR

BORN: *August 23, 1944, Fajardo*

Antonia Novello studied medicine in Puerto Rico, then went to the United States during the early 1970s. She taught pediatrics — children's medicine — at Georgetown University in Washington, D.C. Novello was particularly concerned with treating children with AIDS. In 1989, President George Bush asked her to serve as U.S. Surgeon General, the president's main adviser on health issues. Novello was

the first woman and the first Hispanic to hold that position. After leaving government service in 1993, Novello worked briefly for the United Nations and taught. In 1999, New York governor George Pataki named her the public health commissioner for the state.

Fast Facts

American Samoa (AS)

American Samoa is made up of seven small islands that belong to a larger group of Samoan islands. Located in the southern Pacific Ocean, American Samoa is 2,300 miles (3,700 km) southwest of Honolulu, Hawaii. The islands are the only U.S. territory south of the equator.

The U.S. Navy took control of the island of Tutuila in 1900, and neighboring islands came under U.S. control during the next few years. The native people of American Samoa and other South Pacific islands are Polynesian. Samoan, a Polynesian language, and English are both spoken on the islands. Most of the residents are native Samoans, with some whites, Asians, and natives of the nearby island of Tonga. Major industries include tourism and the processing of tuna. Chief crops are vegetables, nuts, and fruit.

Became U.S. Territory

February 16, 1900

Capital	Population
Pago Pago (Tutuila)	4,278

Total Population (2000)

57,291 — *Between 1990 and 2000, American Samoa's population increased 22 percent.*

Major Counties	Population
Tualauta	22,025
Ma'oputasi	11,695
Lealataua	5,684
Ituau	4,312
Sua	3,417

Land Area

77 square miles (199 sq km)

Motto

"Samoa Muamua le Atua" — *Samoan for "In Samoa, God is first."*

Official Anthem

"Amerika Samoa" *by Napoleon Andrew Tuiteleleapaga and Mariota Tiumalu Tuiasosopo; adopted in 1950.*

Official Plant

Ava — *Also called kava, the roots of the plant are used to make a drink that plays an important role in social and religious events in American Samoa. Ava is also used as a medicine to lower tension.*

Official Flower

Paogo — *Also called ula-fala*

Place to Visit

Fagatele Bay National Marine Sanctuary, Tutuila — *Fagatele Bay is home to many tropical fish, such as the parrot fish and butterfly fish. From June to September, humpback whales play in the warm ocean waters.*

Fast Facts

Commonwealth of the Northern Mariana Islands (CNMI)

The Northern Mariana Islands include the main islands of Saipan, Tinian, Rota, and several smaller islands. They are part of a group of islands in the Pacific Ocean called Micronesia. The Northern Mariana Islands are west of the International Date Line, so they are one day ahead of the United States. They are just north of Guam and share a similar history and culture with that U.S. territory.

The United States took control of the Northern Mariana Islands during World War II, then ruled them through an arrangement worked out with the United Nations. Gradually, the U.S. government gave the Northern Mariana Islands more control over their own affairs. Major industries are trade, services, and tourism. Fruits and vegetables are the main crops.

As in Guam, the first residents of the islands were the Chamorro. Today, Asians make up the largest percentage of the population. English and Chamorro are spoken, as well as Carolinian, a Micronesian language.

Became a Commonwealth
November 3, 1986

Capital	Population
Saipan	62,392

Total Population (2000)
69,221 — *Between 1990 and 2000, the Northern Mariana Islands' population increased 60 percent.*

Major Islands	Population
Saipan	62,392
Tinian	3,540
Rota	3,283

Land Area
179 square miles (464 sq km)

Official Anthem
"Gi Talo Gi Halom Tasi" *in Chamorro,* "Satil Matawal Pacifico" *in Carolinian; adopted in 1996.*

Place to Visit
American Memorial Park, Saipan — *During World War II, Saipan was the site of a bloody battle between U.S. and Japanese forces. Today, American Memorial Park honors the U.S. soldiers and Saipan civilians who died during the fighting. Run by the National Park Service and the government of the Northern Mariana Islands, the park has a memorial listing more than five thousand people who died during the fighting here and on nearby islands. American Memorial Park also has vast grounds where residents and visitors can jog, play tennis, swim, and attend concerts.*

Fast Facts

Guam (GU)

Guam is the largest of the Marianas, an island chain in the western Pacific Ocean located 3,700 miles (5,950 km) west of Hawaii. The island is west of the International Date Line, making it one day ahead of the United States.

After the Spanish-American War, Guam was one of the former Spanish territories that came under U.S. control, along with the Philippines and Puerto Rico. During World War II, Japan occupied the island for almost three years. Since then, the U.S. military has kept several bases on the island, and government work is an important source of jobs for Guamanians. Other important industries are tourism and construction. Assorted vegetables and fruits are the island's main crops.

Guam's first residents were the Chamorro. Today's residents are mostly Filipino, Chamorro, and Caucasian. The Chamorro language, English, and Japanese are spoken on the island.

Became U.S. Territory
December 10, 1898

Capital   Population
Hagatña 1,100

Total Population (2000)
154,805 — *Between 1990 and 2000, Guam's population increased 16 percent*

Major Districts   Population
Dededo 42,980
Yigo 19,474
Tamuning 18,012
Mangilao 13,313
Barrigada 8,652

Land Area
210 square miles (544 sq km)

Motto
"Where America's Day Begins"

Official Anthem
"Stand Ye Guamanians," *also called* "The Guam Hymn," *by Ramon Manalisay Sablan; adopted in 1919.*

Official Bird
tottot — *Also Mariana fruit dove.*

Official Flower
puti tai nobio — *Also bougainvillea*

Place to Visit
Cocos Island — *A small island off the southern coast of Guam, Cocos Island is a popular spot for swimming, sunbathing, and picnicking. A seventeenth-century Spanish ship carrying gold, silver, and jewels sank near the island, and divers are now searching its waters for the treasure.*

Fast Facts

U.S. Virgin Islands (VI)

The U.S. Virgin Islands include St. Thomas, St. Croix, St. John, and fifty smaller islands located 70 miles (113 km) east of Puerto Rico. The United States purchased the islands from Denmark for $25 million in 1917. The major industries in the Virgin Islands are tourism and the production of rum, textiles, and petroleum products. Crops include vegetables and ornamental plants. Most residents are African American or Hispanic. English is the official language, but Spanish, French, and Creole — a West Indian language — are also spoken.

Became U.S. Territory

March 31, 1917

Capital	Population
Charlotte Amalie (St. Thomas)	11,000

Total Population (2000)

108,612 — *Between 1990 and 2000, the Virgin Islands' population increased 7 percent.*

Major Islands	Population
St. Croix	53,234
St. Thomas	51,181
St. John	4,197

Major Towns	Population
Charlotte Amalie	11,004
Christiansted	2,637
Frederiksted	732

Land Area

134 square miles (347 sq km)

Official Anthem

"Virgin Islands March" *by Alton A. Adams; adopted in 1963. The words for this song were taken from suggestions made by the public, then set to a tune by Adams, a native of St. Thomas and the first African American to serve as a bandmaster in the U.S. Navy.*

Official Bird

Yellow breast — *Also called sugar bird and banana quit*

Official Flower

Yellow elder — *Also called yellow cedar or yellow trumpet.*

Place to Visit

Virgin Islands National Park — *This national park covers more than half of St. John and also includes Hassell Island, located off St. Thomas. On St. John, visitors explore the remains of Danish colonial buildings and see items once used by the Carib who lived on the island when European settlers first arrived. The park also features tropical forests and beautiful bays filled with coral reefs.*

Puerto Rico
and Other Outlying Areas
History At-A-Glance

1493
Christopher Columbus claims Puerto Rico for Spain.

1508
Juan Ponce de León leads the first Spanish settlement.

1511
Taíno Indians rebel against Spanish rule.

1518
Spain allows African slaves to be brought to the island for the first time.

1521
The city of San Juan is founded.

1539
Construction begins on El Morro Fortress.

1625
Dutch forces attack Puerto Rico.

1809
Puerto Rico elects its first representative to the Spanish Cortes.

1868
A failed rebellion for independence takes place in Lares.

1873
Slavery is abolished.

1898
Puerto Ricans form their first independent government; the U.S. government takes control of the island.

1898
Guam becomes a U.S. territory.

1600   **1700**   **1800**

1492
Christopher Columbus comes to New World.

1607
Capt. John Smith and three ships land on Virginia coast and start first English settlement in New World — Jamestown.

1754–63
French and Indian War.

1773
Boston Tea Party.

1776
Declaration of Independence adopted July 4.

1777
Articles of Confederation adopted by Continental Congress.

1787
U.S. Constitution written.

1812–14
War of 1812.

United States
History At-A-Glance

1900
The Foraker Act establishes U.S. civilian control over Puerto Rico.

1900
American Samoa becomes a U.S. territory.

1917
The United States purchases the Virgin Islands from Denmark.

1948
For the first time ever, Puerto Ricans elect their own governor, Luis Muñoz Marín.

1952
Puerto Rico votes to become a U.S. commonwealth.

1967
Puerto Rican voters choose to keep the island's commonwealth status.

1972
Baseball star Roberto Clemente dies in a plane crash.

1976
The U.S. Congress changes tax laws to benefit U.S. companies in Puerto Rico.

1986
The Northern Mariana Islands become a commonwealth.

1993
Puerto Rican voters once again choose to keep commonwealth status.

1998
Hurricane Georges causes heavy damage in Puerto Rico; voters again choose to keep commonwealth status.

2000
Sila Calderon becomes the first female governor of Puerto Rico.

1800 | **1900** | **2000**

1848
Gold discovered in California draws eighty thousand prospectors in the 1849 Gold Rush.

1861–65
Civil War.

1869
Transcontinental railroad completed.

1917–18
U.S. involvement in World War I.

1929
Stock market crash ushers in Great Depression.

1941–45
U.S. involvement in World War II.

1950–53
U.S. fights in the Korean War.

1964–73
U.S. involvement in Vietnam War.

2000
George W. Bush wins the closest presidential election in history.

2001
A terrorist attack in which four hijacked airliners crash into New York City's World Trade Center, the Pentagon, and farmland in western Pennsylvania leaves thousands dead or injured.

▼ The city and harbor of Ponce as it looked in the 1890s.

Festivals and Fun for All

Artisans' Fair,
Barranquitas

Each July, craftspeople from across Puerto Rico come to Barranquitas to sell their products.
agueybana.net/Pages/
Catagory%20pages/
What's%20Happening.htm

Casals Festival, San Juan

Founded in 1957 by the great cellist, Pablo Casals, this two-week-long festival celebrates a variety of classical music by local and international musicians.
www.usairways.com/travel/destinations/
caribbean/calendar_location.htm#SanJuan

Coffee Harvest Festival, Maricao

Maricao celebrates the coffee crop each February. Visitors listen to folk music, view crafts, and learn new coffee recipes.
http://www.puertoricoinfo.com/yrevents.htm#top

Discovery Day, Island-wide

One of Puerto Rico's most important holidays is November 19 — Discovery Day, honoring the day Christopher Columbus first landed on the island. Parades, food, and other festivities are featured.
http://www.puertoricanlife.com/
article1031.html

Fiesta de Santiago Apostól, Loíza

Each July, the Loíza's citizens honor St. James with a ten-day party. Music, dances, and colorful masks reflect Puerto Rico's African culture.
www.prfrogui.com/home/loizacar.htm

Hatillo Mask Festival,
Hatillo

Each December, residents of Hatillo act out the Biblical story of King Herod. Sometimes called Holy Innocents Day, the Hatillo festival also includes food, music, and crafts.
www.carlsontravel.com/
Destinations/Puerto_Rico/
puertorico1.htm

Jazz Fest, San Juan

Since 1991, some of the world's top jazz musicians have appeared at this annual late spring festival. The concerts emphasize Latin jazz, which mixes the rhythms of Latin American music with traditional jazz instruments, and "jams," or long solos.
www.prheinekenjazz.com/

Mavi Carnival, Juana Díaz

Juana Díaz was once famous for its sugarcane and coffee beans. Today it is known for its marble — and this April celebration. Mavi is a drink made from the bark of the ironwood tree. The festival features food, parades, and dancing. travel.yahoo.com/p/travelguide/92318

Ponce Carnival, Ponce

This pre-Lenten Carnival is one of the best in Puerto Rico. Large floats, fancy masks, and plenty of dancing add to the festivities. www.elcoquigifts.com/maskvejigante1.asp

Puerto Rico International Regatta, Fajardo

Each March, sailing ships of all sizes compete off Fajardo, the center for pleasure boating in Puerto Rico. After the regatta, or series of boat races, everyone comes ashore for local food, music, and dancing. www.printernationalregatta.com/ notice_of_regatta.html

San Blas Half Marathon, Coamo

The San Blas Half Marathon attracts some of the world's top long-distance runners. A hilly 13.1-mile (21.1-km) course challenges runners. The race is part of a festival that honors the town's patron saint. welcome.topuertorico.org/ city/coamo.shtml

San Juan Bautista Day, San Juan

Puerto Rico's first Spanish name was San Juan Bautista — St. John the Baptist. Many towns celebrate this day, but San Juan's June 24 party is the biggest bash of all. At midnight, people walk backward into the sea three times, which is supposed to bring them good luck. www.festivals.com/01-01-january/ patronsaint/endeavor.cfm

Sugar Cane Festival, San Germán

The second town founded by the Spanish, San Germán celebrates with a weeklong sugarcane festival each April. It features traditional foods, dancing, and music. travel.yahoo.com/p/travelguide/92315

Three Kings Day, Island-wide

Puerto Ricans, like many Hispanics, celebrate a Roman Catholic holiday on the sixth of January called Epiphany, or Three Kings Day. At festivities across the island, men dress as the Three Wise Men who brought gifts to the infant Jesus. The modern-day kings distribute gifts to local children, and families gather for holiday meals. www.puertorico-herald.org/issues/2001/ vol5n49/HolidayTrad-en.shtml

▶ Along with their own festivals and holidays, Puerto Ricans celebrate the U.S. Independence Day, July 4, with parades and dancing.

Books

Bernier-Grand, Carmen T. *Shake It, Morena! And Other Folklore from Puerto Rico*. Brookfield, CT: Millbrook Press, 2002. The author recounts stories, songs, and riddles she learned growing up in Puerto Rico.

Harlan, Julia. *Puerto Rico: Deciding Its Future*. New York: Twenty-First Century Books, 1996. Examines the issue of statehood for Puerto Rico and the concerns of islanders who move to the United States.

Manning, Ruth. *Juan Ponce de León*. Chicago: Heinemann Library, 2000. A biography of the explorer who led the first Spanish settlement in Puerto Rico.

Silva Lee, Alfonso. *Coquí and His Friends: The Animals of Puerto Rico*. St. Paul: Pangaea, 2000. A description of some of the hundreds of animals found in Puerto Rico, written in both English and Spanish.

Web Sites

▶ El Boricua, a cultural web site.
www.elboricua.com/index.html

▶ Puerto Rico Herald: news and political issues.
www.puertorico-herald.org

▶ Welcome to Puerto Rico: people, geography, history, and tourist information.
http://welcome.topuertorico.org

▶ Government to Guam: culture, geography, and people.
http://ns.gov.gu

▶ Commonwealth of the Northern Mariana Islands Government: people, geography, and tourist information.
www.mariana-islands.gov.mp

▶ Office of the Governor of American Samoa: history and events.
www.asg-gov.com

Videos

Puerto Ricans. Schlessinger Media 1993. A look at Puerto Ricans who have moved to the United States.

Puerto Rico: History and Culture. Video Knowledge Learning Library, 2000. History and cultural traditions in Puerto Rico.